NEW YEAR RESOLUTION

AN OPTION FOR CHANGE

NILAM PATHAK

Made with ♥ on the Notion Press Platform
www.notionpress.com

Dedicated to all those who what to use the power of New Year
Resolution to transform themselves.

Contents

Preface

New Year's resolution is an overused word, and we have rarely seen success in it. Somehow in our heart we all know that new year is full of possibilities, and it has the potential to bring drastic positive changes in our lives. But we do not know how. Can there be a way to really understand the concept of New Year's resolution? Can someone present a powerful, but simple technique to create the right New Year's resolution?

The next big challenge is about the execution. Even if we have created the right New Year's resolution, it is rarely executed. It means that the expected outcomes from the resolutions are not achieved. People after repeated failures either stop making the New Year's resolutions, or make it only for fun.

It is a missed opportunity, which has the potential to transform our lives completely.

The objective of this book is to create champions in the concept of New Year's resolutions and direct the energy and resources of the readers in the right direction so that they can achieve the expected results from their New Year's resolutions.

We have discussed powerful ideas and effective techniques to support people in unleashing the power from their New Year's resolution. If the readers sincerely follow the techniques and the steps specified in the book, then they can transform their New Year's resolution into a big opportunity, which is full of possibilities and hope.

Readers workbook attached with the chapters of the book to facilitate the development of their New Year's resolution, its evaluation, and execution.

We are sure that after completion of this book the readers will have powerful tools at their disposal to bring the desired changes in their lives, to become more successful, satisfied, and happy.

CHAPTER ONE

Introduction

Every New Year brings an opportunity for transformation for all, but few people know about it. In this book, we will learn this secret and utilize it to get success in life and work.

We all have seen people getting **excited about the new year**. They celebrate with their families and friends to welcome the start of the year. This is irrespective of region, language, religion, skin color or financial status. We all eagerly wait for 12 o'clock in the night, when the last year ends and the new year starts. Why is that?

The new year is full of possibilities and hope. It brings freshness and newness to the lives of people, even though the people and the conditions around them remain same. With the start of new year, we hope to solve our problems and resolve long pending issues to get peace of mind. We also look for the possibilities of doing something unique and great, which can change our lives drastically. A new year brings with itself enough number of hours, to get things done.

Even if everything remains same, the people, their problems, environment, complexities of life and their relationship with others, we all welcome the new year with enthusiasm. It is not about the condition of people, but about their mental state. A new year means something new, fresh, and full of hope. We find it positive, which is going to suck out negativity from our lives. We find new year different, which has the potential to bring happiness and success to our lives. **We consider previous year as the past** in which we have left our weaknesses, complexities, and difficulties of life and work, **while the new year is the future,** which we can design it as we want. Past year looks out of our control, while new year looks in our control. We embrace the coming year with open hands and an expectation of great personal life and exciting work.

Due to these reasons, people find a lot of motivation to take challenges in the new year. New year resolution is the product of it. People make several New Year's resolutions to bring drastic changes to their lives, work, health, finance, and relationships. Everything looks great and exciting before the start of new year, but once the new year starts, we find it hard to follow our resolutions. This story repeats every year. It is not about one year or two years, but every year. Why people make New Year's resolutions every year, but are unable to follow or get the required outcomes out of them? It looks frustrating, but again there is New Year, around the corner.

This book will try to solve the problem of failing in NY Resolutions. We will make the right New Year's resolution, and then follow them to achieve our goals. We have discussed powerful ideas and an effective methodology to allow you to guide your thinking process and direct your energy towards making the right New Year's resolutions, for yourself and to get success in those resolutions.

Objective of the Book

The objectives with which this book is written.

- To make you **understand the truth about the New Year's resolution** so that its power can be unleashed.
- To guide you **to make the right New Year's resolutions** for yourself, with a logical methodology.
- **To make you focus your energy** on the implementation of the actions, for achieving the required outcomes, from your New Year's resolution.
- Finally, to **support you in making your own system for New Year's resolutions,** so that you get success in coming years consistently.

Who would need this book?

Let's talk about the people for whom this book is designed and developed.

- **If you are looking for the right way to make the New Year's Resolution** which can add to your success, then this book is for you for bringing clarity to your mind.
- If you think that the start of new year is nothing but a boring next day, then this book can help you **to make your next year as transformative** for yourself.
- **If you are looking for consistent growth** in your life, then this book can help.
- If you are among those people who have previously made New Year's resolutions, but have **failed**, and are looking for logical ways to make it a success, then you should take this book.

What can you expect after completing this book

- You will **understand the logic of** New Year's **Resolution**.
- You will develop skills to **create the right** New Year's **Resolution** for yourself, which will work.
- You will be equipped to **help others to succeedin their** New **Year Resolutions**.

What is expected from the readers

- The readers have the freedom to take the book as they want, but it would be beneficial that they **follow the flow of the book**. Once the book is complete, they can choose any topic to reinforce the concepts by reading to specific chapters again.
- It would be important to **complete the book,** as all the topics and ideas are synergistically connected to each other.
- We expect readers to **do all the exercises and follow the instructions** as specified in each lecture, which would allow them to strengthen their concepts.
- This book is to build the fundamentals of developing and executing New Year's Resolution. **Keep learning and succeeding** in your resolutions and goals by getting feedback and improving on your weak areas.

Basic qualification required for the book

- There is **no minimum qualification** required for this book, anyone who wants to understand about making the New Year's Resolution and keeping them to get the required outcomes, can learn from this book.
- The book is written in English, therefore you need to **understand English,** to get the value out of this book.
- You need to be committed enough **to complete the book and do its exercises** with complete sincerity.

How to do it

- To get the maximum value out of this book, you need to start from the beginning and move step by step forward. **Follow the book with its flow**. This is important, as to understand a topic, you need to get clarity on its previous topics.
- It is required that you **follow the instructions as specified** in each section. Following the instructions would help you to become a better learner.
- It is suggested that even if you have some brief understanding about a specific portion, it would be beneficial that you **complete those topics in the book.** It would act like the good revision for the topic or idea, and act as an opportunity to build a momentum for completing the book.
- You need to **keep practicing** by making new resolutions and getting success. The more you do it the better you will become at it

Index and flow of the book

The book's structure and its flow:

In the initial portion of the book, we will educate you about **the concept of New Year's Resolution** and the related topics. This would include general reasons for people making New Year's Resolutions, success rate and why most of the people are not able to follow their resolutions. We will also cover **most popular New Year's Resolutions** made by people in the past years, advantages and disadvantages of making New Year's Resolutions.

The next part of the book we will try to answer "**Should you make resolutions?**" We will then guide you through the process of finding your resolutions and then checking it for its genuineness. We will also identify the various **strategies for keeping the resolutions to get results.** In this portion, we will also discuss the different ways to develop "**resolution mindset**".

Finally, we will suggest you the **commonly made New Year's Resolutions to ease your process of identifying your own New Year's Resolution.**

CHAPTER TWO

New Year Resolution

We all have the option to choose the New Year's resolution as either "Something, which everybody is making and it is in fashion" or it can be an "Opportunity for transformation". If you want to get value out of your New Year's Resolution by keeping them and achieving the required outcomes, then it must be considered as an opportunity, in which you can create value for yourselves and for others. If you are not serious about your New Year's resolution, then it would be better to not make it, as it would do more damage than giving you any value.

Let us now understand the concept and logic behind the success of New Year's Resolutions.

What is a Resolution?

The meaning of resolution is "A decision to do something or to behave in a certain manner". It is **a commitment to behave or act in a certain way for some specific benefits.**

To keep space clutter-free on the pages, we will **write New Year Resolution as NYR.**

- **NYR – Can it be transformative**: Generally, people make lots of resolutions in their lives to either improve in some areas, to leave a bad habit or for a specific gain. The most popular is the "New Year's Resolution" which a large number humanity makes before the start of a new year. It is generally the commitment to self about behaving in a certain way or doing something. It has become a fashion to make New Year's Resolutions with high hopes, even without any intention to follow it. If you can understand the power of "New Year's Resolution", then it can act as a **transformative** moment, in which you develop yourself and become better. There are examples of the people who have utilized the New Year's Resolution as the force to bring a winning change in themselves, their families and in their organizations. For example, a "New Year's Resolution to never lose temper" can bring a drastic improvement in the relationships. A resolution to stop smoking can bring visible improvements in the health of a person. The only thing required is the clarity, commitment, and discipline.

- Resolution is a **firm decision** by an individual to act and behave in a certain way, without exceptions. The resolution has certain outcomes, which the individual making it, desires. An individual can make a resolution at any time of the year, or month or day, which means that he has decided on something, with which he is completely convinced. Any resolution should have **certain benefits for the person** and other people associated with him. Even though "New Year's Resolution" is most popular, but we can **make a resolution at any time by taking a decision.**

- Generally, **resolutions are not forced, instead, they are self-decided**. Resolution is a personal decision, which cannot be forced or decided by somebody else. It must be self-decided and committed. If the resolution is forced, then the individual would lack **commitment** towards it. Without commitment, it is difficult to act with strength. Most of the forced decisions have difficulties in implementation.

- Resolution is **specified in words,** which can exist in an appropriately written format or exist in thoughts. Though, writing down your resolution is always a better option, than just thinking about it. A written down resolution brings clarity to the mind about its purpose and the outcomes to be achieved.

- **Few people are serious about New Year's resolutions**, while most of the people do it "just for doing". These people are not seriously interested in changing themselves, instead, they want to be part of the group of people, who are making the resolutions and declaring it openly. They do not want to be the odd man amongst the people making New Year's resolutions.

- Resolution can also be considered as an agreement between the members of a team or teams to act and behave in a certain way. It is an agreement about a specific decision. It means that specific roles have been decided, and everybody associated needs to follow it strictly. It is the **decision taken by the group or team** for a specific action, to get the required outcomes.

- **An organization, association or an institution can also make "New Year's Resolution"**. Just like a team, they can decide on a specific rule to be followed to bring improvements and growth. For example, a hotel's management and staff can decide to act and behave in all required ways to delight their customers and get the five-star rating.

Data about New Year Resolution

Now, let us look at some data and information to understand how others are doing in their New Year Resolutions.

Most commonly made New Year Resolutions

1. Lose Weight and Get Fit
2. Quit Smoking
3. Learn Something New
4. Eat Healthier and Diet
5. Get Out of Debt and Save Money
6. Spend More Time with Family
7. Travel to New Places
8. Be Less Stressed
9. Volunteer
10. Drink Less

People keeping their New Year Resolution

Thirty-five percent of people who make New Year's resolutions break them by the end of January. Out of these only 30% will keep their resolution.

It means that only 20% of those who make a resolution will see it through to completion.

Finally, only a smaller percentage of initial people, who made the New Year's Resolution, will get the desired outcomes.

More NYR Data

- Generally, 1/3 of the educated adults make NYR.
- Out of these 20% would be fitness & health goals.
- 15% would be for education, skills and hobby goals.
- Only around 20% of the people think that they can keep their resolution by the end of the year.
- 2-5% of people would leave their resolution within the first week of new year.
- 50% will leave in first three months.

CHAPTER THREE

Birth of a Resolution

There are some specific basic reasons for making any resolution, including New Year's Resolution. It can either be to gain something or to get rid of something or it can be due to peer pressure. Let's look at these fundamental forces giving birth to New Year's Resolutions.

Pain-

If something is disturbing or upsetting somebody in some way, then that person would decide to deal with it. A resolution takes birth. **A pain can be a problem, a fear, a weakness, frustration, or sorrow which compels a person to take action. The severity of the pain can activate the will-power** of the person to take required decisions, even if they were pending for a long time. Once the decision is taken and outcomes are decided, the individual would act on it to **relieve his pain**. For example, a person frustrated by the taunts of people for failure can make "a New Year's Resolution" to take massive action for creating a successful business. His pain from the frustration would be the driving force for his action. This **driving force may weaken or even dies down**, when the pain is reduced or becomes negligible.

Pleasure-

A pleasure is "**a feeling of enjoyment, happiness, and satisfaction**". Everybody desires it. If a person expects **to get something pleasurable for achieving specific results,** then he needs to take a decision on it. A resolution takes birth. A pleasure is the desire to get something. The quest for money, fame and power is due to the need for pleasure. It is assumed by most of the people that wealth and influence can be a big source of pleasure. They believe that these elements are directly related, but that is not always the case. Money can only be one of the medium for pleasure. The need for pleasure **makes people toil (work hard) and persevere**, but also sometimes compels them to take immoral and even illegal actions to get the desired outcomes. A wrong path to pleasure would always lead to pain.

<u>Influence</u>-

Influence of the **peer groups** is the most common factor, as many social influencers are making their New Year's resolutions. Through data analysis, it can be considered as the biggest group, which makes "New Year's resolution". People are influenced by their peers, teams, and groups to make the New Year's resolution, even if they do not want it. They do it **to remain in synchronization with their group,** in which almost everybody is making their "New Year's resolution".

<u>Hope</u> –

Hope is a powerful concept for every human being.

Meaning: "**It is a feeling of expectation and desire for a particular thing to happen**".

A hopeful sentence would be "The next year would be different and better than the previous one, and I can achieve my long pending goals."

Hope can be a great motivator to take complex decisions and tough actions. Some people make "New Year's Resolution" with a hope in their mind to achieve something or for some specific fulfillment. It should also be understood that only hope would not deliver results, strong actions must back it.

What it is not?

We should also understand what "New Year's resolution" is not. Many time we confuse NYR with something completely different. To get success in our NYR we should be aware of them.

Do not confuse NYR with...

A resolution for new year means action, not only words-

Our resolution has expectations about specific outcomes, which would require decisions and powerful actions. Resolution is not only a set of words or phrases, instead, it is a commitment backed by beliefs and actions. If your resolution for the new year remains only in words, without any action, then you are deceiving yourself. You must make the commitment for the new year only when you are serious about it and ready to put efforts to it.

A variable resolution-

Your "New Year's Resolution" should be fixed, not variable. Your commitment to something should not change every day or week. To fulfill the commitment, you need to put your focus and energy towards it and put efforts into its preparations. If you keep changing your New Year's Resolution then it would be confusing to your mind and you will not be able to focus on it to achieve results. If you are not clear about your resolution for the new year, wait until you have clarity.

A desire, without will-power to act-

We all have a lot of desires in our life. Some of these desires are achievable, while most of them are unachievable, due to their impracticality and irrationality. If your "New Year's Resolution" remains only a desire, without the commitment to act, then it is the wastage of time and energy. In that case, it is better not to make any resolution for New Year.

A goal without 'Why'-

"Why" is a powerful word, which provides you with the reason for a specific action. Answering "why" gives you the clarity in your mind about the reasons and logic behind your actions. "Why" also gives you the emotional connection with the cause, goal, and objective. For "New Year's Resolution", you must have the clarity about your "Why?", without which you should not be making the resolution for the new year.

A direction without clarity-

If we do not have a direction, we are lost. A goal allows us to focus our energy and action towards a specific direction, without which our efforts and energy would be wasted, without the outcomes. For "New Year's Resolution" you must have a clear goal and the direction to follow. In no case you should be having two resolutions for the new year, pointing in different directions.

A job without emotional connection-

If you are not emotionally connected to your goal, then you would find resistance to follow it. You must invest enough time to connect with the resolution, which you are making for the new year so that you give it sincerity and attention.

CHAPTER FOUR

Why people make NYR?

Why are people making NYR? What are they trying to get out of it? What are their genuine objectives? In this section, we will answer these questions. Every NYR has a specific objective attached to it. Even similar resolution may have different objectives. You also need to know your objective of making NYR. Is it strong enough?

<u>Change</u>: Some individuals want **to bring some specific change** in themselves and in their lives. For example, you may want to improve your health and get fit in the next year. In some cases, people have the resolutions for the new year to bring change in someone else or something. For instance, you may want to modify the culture of your organization slightly, by making it your "New Year's Resolution."

<u>Skills and competencies</u> are an important part of career success. Many people focus their "New Year's Resolution" towards **enhancing their skills and competencies** in some specific area. It is a great opportunity to think afresh and develop yourself and your career in the process.

<u>Growth</u> is an important element for satisfaction in life. Without growth, you may feel stuck and outdated. An

individual may make "a New Year's Resolution" to grow in life and work by taking the required actions towards it.

Weaknesses: Everybody has weaknesses, but only minority of the people take actions towards limiting them. New Year can be a great starting point **to work on your weaknesses** to either weaken them or eliminate them. For example, an individual can decide to leave smoking to improve his health. It is to be noted that you should not be choosing several weaknesses simultaneously, instead you should choose only one weakness and move to next, only after getting success in the previous one.

Develop Strengths: We all want to **develop different strengths** for success in our life and work. We all know that people with more competencies have better chances of success in their life. New Year can be a great opportunity to develop new strengths, and strengthen the existing ones. Identify a strength which you want to develop, make the "New Year's Resolution" and make it one of your strength.

Take Decisions: We all have several **long-pending decisions and actions,** which are waiting for months or even years. New Year can be a great opportunity to deal with them. For some, it is an opportunity to move forward in a specific decision or action on New Year, by making it as their resolution.

Fulfil Commitment: Many times, people make commitments, but they are unable to follow through. Most of these people have the feeling of guilt for not honoring their commitment. People utilize the start of New Year **to fulfill their commitment**. For example, New Year can be a good opportunity to visit your friends and honor your commitment to meet them.

Start Fresh: Many times, we are trapped in the complexities of life. Sometimes, it can get so twisted that it looks almost impossible to unwind and get out of it. Some people get into a downward spiral of emotions and stress. Sometimes, we may feel suffocated without finding any crack to escape. A new year can be a great start **to start fresh**. We can even take this opportunity to start our job, work, or anything else on a complete blank paper.

Miracle: Some people make New Year's resolutions in the **hope for a miracle**. These people may not have any intention of acting on the resolution, instead, they are hoping for magic to do the job for them. These people need to wake up and face the reality.

To deal with a nagging problem: You may have a big problem to solve but are unable to find the solution. Your lack of attention towards it could be the reason. Utilize the new year **to solve your problem** with an objective to get rid of it, with a clear solution.

To take firm decisions: It is the truth that many people are confused in their life and are unable to make decisions. New Year can be a great starting point to bring clarity to your mind and **take firm decisions**. To do it, you can start with one simple decision, which you can take immediately. Decisions have value, only when they are acted upon with sincerity.

Why people make resolution only in New Year?

It is a fresh start after ending the previous year. At the end of the year, we may feel the heaviness of past days, which were full of challenges and complexities. New Year looks fresh, energetic, and full of hope. People look towards the start of the year with great expectations, that is the reason they celebrate for it.

People are generally positive about their next year. It is a known fact that people are generally positive about the next year than the previous ones. It is due to the effect of hope and their self-confidence on themselves, to get success in their actions. Everybody knows that they have the power to modify the book of their life, by bringing required changes in their behavior and actions. New Year looks a great opportunity to utilize your authority for bringing the positive changes in your life. It is to be noted that only a few people do it.

People are generally enthusiastic **after Christmas and long year-end holidays.** That is a great time to make resolutions for the new year to bring the long pending change in your life.

It is a **fashion** to make a New Year's Resolution. Everybody is making it. People want to be the part of the crowd by making the resolution ourselves, even without much thinking about it.

It is the **buzz word.** It looks cool to make the New Year's Resolution and broadcast it on social networking sites and on your website.

Psychologically, turn of the year in a moment, looks a big event. Everything changes, it seems that we can change too. Everybody wants something to gain and to change. That can be a great motivator to make the resolution for the new year, to bring that big change.

CHAPTER FIVE

What happens to NYR?

We should understand the truth about NYR. What happens to the large number of people making NYR? Do they get success? If not, what are the reasons for it? We will answer these questions in this section.

As most of the **people are not serious** about making the New Year's Resolution, they are unable to follow it. A big percentage of these people do not even start any action on their resolution. Some of the people, who try to take some action on the resolution, are unable to continue it after two weeks. It means that before the end of January, most of the people who have made the resolution for the new year, have left their resolutions behind.

The start of new year is mainly about the perception of the people about it. The turn of the year creates a positive mental state, for most of the humanity. We need to understand that only the calendar is updated to the new year, while the **environment and the person remain the same.** New Year is a good opportunity to change the mental state, and orient it towards doing something of importance. Some people utilize it to transform themselves completely. Many people making New Year's Resolution are not able to understand this simple concept, that is the reason they fail in their resolutions.

One of the most complex activity for any organization and for an individual is **"change"**. **Change is always difficult**, for an individual, a group, an organization, or a community. Most of the conflicts in the world are due to the rigidness of the people, as they are not ready to change. Our New Year's Resolution may require changes in our thinking, behavior, and actions. It is natural to feel emotional resistance to it. Till we are emotionally ready for pursuing the New Year's Resolution, it would be difficult to take any concrete action for it. Being emotionally ready is difficult, and it may take some time. It means that we need to be proactive for our resolutions and start early.

Most of the people who are making New Year's Resolutions are **not committed to it**. They lack the seriousness of the goals and the true need for outcomes. The results they want are "good to have" or "should have", that is a reason they are unable to get results. Till they move from "should" to "must", they will not be able to act on their resolution. Increase your commitment level, and get results.

Procrastination is a big problem for getting things done. Procrastination is the habit of delaying, postponing the decisions and actions for achieving outcomes. We all do it. Winners have learned the habit of dealing with their procrastination by taking concrete actions, even against their moods and feelings. Losers find their habit of procrastination too big to challenge.

Some people become complacent by getting initial wins. They start to believe too much in their abilities to achieve the results, and therefore their overconfidence degrades their motivation and hence action. We need to be careful about the feeling of **complacency**, which can affect our performance.

Many people make the resolution for the New Year in haste, without thinking much about it. Once in New Year, they are **unable to find the starting point**. They do not know about the actions to be taken, and results to be achieved. They are bewildered, and soon they lose interest in following their resolution.

People try to take action on their resolution **without even planning** for it. Some people mistake it for an easy task, therefore they become complacent about it. They have not planned for it. Without planning we are directionless, which negatively affects the motivation of the person.

The most important element to move forward for an action is motivation. We need to take steps to keep our spirits high. **Initial successes** in any work are a great motivator. If you can get initial success in the work which you are doing, that would give the required push to move forward towards your goals. It is true for getting success in the New Year's Resolutions too. You need to plan for the results of your New Year's Resolution strategically. People who are unable to get initial successes in their New Year Resolution get easily demoralized. Hence, they lose their grip on the resolution.

Making the New Year's Resolution looks exciting and full of energy. A person can feel the rush of adrenaline through their body while declaring their New Year's Resolution to themselves and to others. But after some time, they feel **disconnected** to it. Actions for resolution becomes boring, and they are unable to follow it. Soon, their New Year's Resolution fizzles out. It is necessary to keep the New Year's Resolution as motivating, and its actions exciting. It must be a conscious effort, which means that you need to regularly think about the ways to keep it exciting and act on them.

For some people, their New Year's Resolution proves to be **wrong**. It was made in haste, without thinking much about it. They say "we never wanted it. It is just wrong." Their excuse is expected, that the time of making the resolution and time of its execution is different. That is the reason it looks illogical at the time of action. They quit it, which seems the easiest way out. Leaving the resolution behind is a missed opportunity, instead, it should be modified based on the present conditions and requirements, to make it generate maximum value.

Sometimes people make **big commitments** for their New Year's resolution. For example, the decision to transform themselves can be tough and complex, as it may take several years for people to change themselves. Similarly, any external event which is not in your control, should not be associated with your New Year Resolution. In these cases, the initial failures demoralize the person, making him lose interest in NY resolution, due to its impracticality. We need to be rational while making the New Year's resolution, so that they are attainable and sensible. Also, they should remain interesting and exciting.

Many times, people are unable to follow their resolutions for new year due to **external factors**, which are not in their control. It is possible that the conditions while making the New Year's resolution are completely different from the conditions at the start of New Year. For example, we may have the resolution to achieve the certain financial target for our organization, but due to economic depression, those initial goals may look unachievable. We cannot do much about the external factors, only we need to modify our resolution slightly to suit the environment and the present realities.

Sometimes people commit massive goals, which are **unachievable within the available time**, competences, and resources. Once the reality sets in, people get demoralized. Your goals need to be rational, neither too easy not too hard.

There are two types of people, externally-driven, and internally-driven. Most of the humanity is **extremely-driven**, which means that they need external stimulus and energy to act and move forward. A smaller percentage of the people are internally-driven, which means that they are self-driven and do not require any external motivation for action. Externally-driven people find it difficult to follow their New Year's Resolution, as their energy is borrowed from outside. As the source of their enthusiasm leaves them, their resolution falls apart. They are unable to follow it. The only solution to this problem is to either find a reliable partner for making your resolution a success, or you should become an **internally-driven** person in which you are the source of energy and motivation for yourself.

Simplicity is a powerful idea to follow. If you keep your tasks and activities simple, you can focus on actions to get results. If the task becomes complex, then you tend to get lost in its twisted maze. The actions for your resolution must be simple to follow. If you get complexity in your actions, then following the resolution for New Year becomes difficult. It should be understood that the actions for the resolution are an additional activity in your daily life. They may be bothering sometimes. Therefore, it is a good idea to keep the activities simple, so that you follow them to get the required results.

Our **actions are guided by our thoughts**. If both are pointing in a different direction, then we cannot focus.

For some people their thoughts and their actions differ, therefore, they find it difficult to follow their resolutions and achieve their goals. The simple solution to this problem is to respect your ideas and allow your actions to follow your decisions and thinking.

Weakness in action is the biggest problem for not getting results. People either act half-heartedly or **do not take action**. This is the difference between the winners and losers. Winners act, while losers keep thinking about action, but never move forward. Either they are too confused or too afraid to act. It should be understood that New Year's Resolution would require clear decisions and tough actions to get the desired outcomes out of your resolutions. The best way to do it is to take an initial action immediately, without thinking much about it. Once you get into the mode of taking actions for required outcomes, then you can build momentum towards your goals.

Perfection is a great way of thinking, but it should not affect your ability to get results. There is a minute difference between excellence and perfection, but if you waste a lot of time in getting perfection, then you can miss opportunities, which do not wait for anybody. You should strive for perfection, but rationally. Many people who are unable to follow their resolutions of New Year keep waiting for perfection to happen. Perfection either never happens or takes a lot of time to materialize. Many irrational perfectionists keep waiting without getting success in the resolutions. Your objective is to get the quality outcomes. You must move forward by taking sincere action in getting results. It is logical to be excellent in outcomes, rather than waiting for perfection forever, with zero results.

Strangely, people like to play the blame game in their New Year's Resolution. They would always **blame**

somebody for their failures, for not taking any action or for not getting results. It is a habit and they would always do it. But they are unable to understand that by blaming others for their failures, is eventually making them a failure. The solution is to stop blaming others and take responsibility for your actions to get results.

People make New Year's Resolutions, but they are **unable to answer 'Why'** for it. 'Why' is an important element for emotionally connecting with your New Year's Resolution. Till you are convinced with it logically and connected with it emotionally, you will not be able to follow your New Year's resolution till the end. Before making your New Year's resolution, introspect and find the 'Why' for it.

Why are people unable to follow it?

Now let us look at some of the reasons, which are responsible for resisting the success in people's New Year Resolutions. Some of these are simple, while others are complex. It is necessary to understand them so that we do not fall into their trap.

What are reasons for failure in NYR?

Where people go wrong? What is the problem?

- They are not **motivated** for taking action, and to achieve their goals.
- They are **confused** about the direction, actions to be taken and results to be achieved.
- They are **externally-driven rather than internally**. It means that external forces push them to action, instead they driving themselves.

- They are **not clear** about their directions and actions. As their New Year Resolution is not clear, their direction is foggy and actions weak.
- They are not **disciplined**. For achieving anything, discipline carries utmost importance. It makes people to behave in the right way, to follow the right rules, and taking all required actions for achieving results.
- The **delay in taking action**. Procrastination is a weapon of losers and un-achievers. They keep delaying their actions by citing strange and funny reasons.
- They are **notready**. They feel that they are not ready to move forward for action. It can be due to lack of competencies or confidence in themselves.
- They **choose the wrong resolution**. Some people start to believe that they have chosen the wrong resolution because they are unable to find any value in it. Their New Year's Resolution was either made in haste or with the influence of others.
- They are not **emotionally connected** to it. They are unable to find the 'Why' for their New Year's Resolution. Without knowing about 'Why' for their New Year's resolution, they cannot be emotionally connected to it. They lack the internal force to drive them forward.
- They do not find it **rational**. Many people find their resolution as Logically wrong. Once people start to take actions on their New Year's Resolutions, they may find logical flaws in it, which puts them off. Their commitment to their New Year's Resolution fizzles out.
- They **lack required skilland competencies**. It is possible that the New Year's Resolutions require some specific skills and competencies to take action. Due to certain individual reasons, required skills were not

developed in time, therefore actions towards their resolutions become impractical.

- They **lack resources and support**. Certain resolutions may require some specific resources and support of certain groups and people. If you are not proactive in planning for your New Year's resolution, then you can hit the roadblock due to lack of certain resources and people.

- People who are not serious about making their New Year's resolution can never take required actions to make it a success. Many people make it "just for making, as everybody is making it". Strangely, a large number of people fall into this category, they just do not know about it.

- They **cannot pull themselves to follow their New Year's Resolution**. They lack the power of will. Willpower is a common energy source, for all actions. Without it, results cannot be achieved. Even your New Year's Resolutions must be backed by your willpower. If you are unable to provide the necessary strength of the will for your New Year's Resolution, then it would be a flop.

Advantages of making the resolutions and keeping them.

- You feel **freshness for a new start** (due to the influence of festive season and holidays). You want to "Start something new".
- It is an **opportunity to change** or even transform yourself.

- You get the **support of other people** to follow through.
- you **learn about yourself** in the process. Even if you try and fail, you learn something about yourself.
- you **learn something new with the actions** you take. There is a high chance that you will develop some new skill. For example, you take a long pending android book to enhance your skills set, to grow in your career.
- You **become better** in some way. When you act or even take a firm decision of doing something, that makes you better.
- It acts as a specific **deadline** to complete pending decisions and action. January 1, can be the day to take a specific decision or action, which is being delayed for a long time.
- It can be good for your **relationships**, if you decide to act on your New Year's Resolution to spend more quality time every week with your family and friends, without fail.
- You can get the **freedom from your bad habits and develop good ones**.
- It is an **opportunity to break the cycle of negativity** and start with freshness and positivity on a new year.

Disadvantages of NYR

- If you regularly make New Year's Resolutions but never follow through, then **it loses value**.
- Lack of seriousness in your New Year's Resolutions would make January 1 as '**just another day**' for you, not the start of anything new. It would seem more like the extension of the previous year.

- It can give you **anxiety** or even stress, due to the deadline of December 31.
- The **pressure** to act on your New Year's Resolution may result in confusion, making you unable to take any decision or right action.
- If you make an unreasonable New Year's Resolution due to peer pressure, but do not follow through, which can make you **lose credibility** in the eyes of others.
- You take a wrong decision and follow it, leading to **unwanted outcomes**.

Should you make resolutions

Should you make the NYR? It is a big question and not easy to answer. Here we will ease the process of answering this question.

To know about your readiness to make the NYR you should take an evaluation test. This test is available in your workbook which you can download in this book.

Before making the NYR you must know about your 'want' and requirements.

Then you should question your:

- Enthusiasm
- Focus
- Commitment
- Discipline
- Flexibility
- Perseverance
- Seriousness.

You can do justice to your NY Resolution only if you are sincere about it.

Test your readiness to make NYR

Let's make this analysis simple and straightforward, through a set of questions.

We should start the evaluation through the first question.

- Is there something which you REALLY want to happen in the new year? If yes, what are they? If no, then do not make the resolution.
- Do you REALLY feel the need/requirement for it?

  - What will happen if that change does not happen?
  - What will happen if that change happens?

- Are you enthusiastic about bringing these changes?
- Are you focused on the results to be achieved?
- Are you ready to take a commitment to it?
- Are you disciplined to follow through?
- Are you flexible to change your plans to get your resolution results?
- Will you persevere even in the face of setbacks and failures?
- What is my seriousness level of my resolution?

CHAPTER SEVEN

Questions for introspection

Now it the time for some introspection. In this section, we will present you with four sets of questions about your Personal Health, Personal Growth, Personal Life and Financial Goals. These question will serve as a starting point to think about your needs and requirements, a necessary starting point before making the NYR.

Personal health

- How would you rate yourself on health factor? Rate yourself on the scale of 1 to 10 (*with 10 as maximum and 1 as minimum*). What are the reasons for this rating?

- What improvements do you require in your health and fitness?

- What according to you will happen if you do not bring these changes in your health?

- How would your life improve if you could bring these changes in your health?

- According to you what actions are required to bring necessary improvements in health and fitness?

- How can you make sure that you take the required actions and maintain them?

Personal growth

- What one skill I should develop that would add maximum value to my work?

- What actions do I need to take to develop this one skill?

- How would I become better professionally, If I could develop this one skill?

- What one strength I should have that could add maximum value to my life and work?

- Which one weakness is responsible for maximum obstruction to my growth and happiness? Why?

- What actions are required to deal with this one weakness?

- How would my life change, if I could get rid of this one weakness?

- How would I like to improve intellectually in the next year?

- What actions must I take for these improvements?

- How would my life be, if I could bring these improvements?

Personal life

- What improvements do I want in my personal life?

- If I must choose one area to change in my life, what it would be?

- What actions do I need to take to bring these changes?

- How would my life improve by bringing these changes?

- What actions must I take to connect better with my loved ones?

- How would my life enhance, if I am able to connect better with my loved ones?

Financial goals

- What financial enhancements do I want in my life?

- If I must choose one (financial enhancement), then what it would be? Why?

- What actions do I need to take to bring the required financial changes in my life?

- How would my life be, if I could achieve my financial goals?

CHAPTER EIGHT

Find your resolution

Can there be a systematic process of identification of NYR? Yes, we have designed it for the people who want to Unleash the Power of their NYR.

In this section, we will learn about the process of identification of NY Resolution and the basic structure of the process.

Process of identification of resolution

We have defined a structure with step by step process of identification of NYR.

This chart shows the basic structure of the whole process to "Find the Resolution".

Basic Structure

Know what you truly want: Before making your New Year's Resolutions you need to know what you want and require in life and work. We all know about it, only we need to focus and discover it. Take some time to think and feel about the requirements of your life, which require decisions and actions.

Prioritize: Generally, people have a long list of their needs and requirements. As you cannot put your energy to all of them simultaneously, therefore it is logical to focus on one specific area to put your full force. To do it right, you need to prioritize your requirements in life and work. It is the individual's choice to choose her New Year's Resolution, but the list of prioritized items would help.

Define your resolution- Once you have identified the area, you need to define it clearly in simple and memorable words. It is a necessary activity, as your New Year's Resolution must be one of the items at the top of your mind.

Plan for it- Next, you need to plan for execution. You have identified your New Year's Resolution, now you should have a proper plan of execution guiding you in your actions, to get the desired outcomes.

Start early to create momentum- You need to create a momentum for your New Year's Resolutions before entering the new year. It is like an object in motion, which is easier to accelerate in comparison to a stationary object. Once you are in speed, it would be better and easier for you to drive it smoothly, even on rough patches on your path. It means that you must start to work on your resolution, by taking initial steps, one or two weeks before the last year ends.

Enter New Year- You should start your new year with powerful action on your resolution and with the commitment to continue it. The initial few days of New Year would be full of excitement, possibilities, and responsibility for your New Year's Resolution. Take its complete responsibility and follow your plan, till you achieve the outcomes.

Get early success- Your plan should include easy activities with simple outcomes and shorter deadlines. You need to focus on getting early successes to add to the momentum for the New Year's Resolution. Initial success would provide necessary motivation, for taking better and stronger actions.

Get more momentum- If you can do any other activity to strengthen the momentum for your New Year's Resolution then go-ahead for it. Every person can identify their own unique way of enhancing the momentum of actions, for keeping a commitment.

Get feedback- Feedback is an important part of constant improvement and growth. You need to self-analyze yourself and take self-feedback. If required you can request feedback from others too, for understanding their perspective about your actions. The next step is to analyze the feedback received and make the required modifications and corrections to your actions.

Implement- Implementation of the ideas generated from the feedback is an important part to get the quality outcomes from your New Year's Resolution. You cannot be hundred percent correct in your initial efforts, therefore you need to keep improving after analyzing your actions and outcomes.

Get results - The final objective is to get results from your New Year's Resolutions. For example, if you have decided to quit smoking, then the outcome would be to quit smoking completely and sustaining it.

Start again- Achieving your New Year's resolution is not the end, instead, it is the starting point of getting success in more goals. It is a great motivator to achieve results and then start again, to take bigger challenges for improving your life and the lives of others.

CHAPTER NINE

Process of Making the NYR

Now is the time to learn about the process of making the NY Resolution. It contains five interlinked parts, with the previous part leading to next. Each part is specified in the form of instruction. You should follow them to develop your right NYR, which will work for you.

How to make your New Year Resolutions

Making your NY Resolution

Part 1

- Is there something which you REALLY want to happen in the new year? List all of them.
- Rate each of them (in strength) on the scale of 1 to 10, with 1 as minimum and 10 as maximum.
- Select the items which have the rating of more than 7.

Rate each of the above in strength, on the scale of 1 to 10, with 1 as minimum and

10 as maximum.

Part 2

- For each item write "Why you want it to happen?" "What will be the outcomes, if that does not happen?"
- Update your rating on these items again, if required.
- Choose one of the items for creating your New Year's Resolution. Specify it in simple, clear words.

Shortlist the items which have the rating more than 7.

For each write "why I want it to happen?" "What will be the outcomes, if that does not

happen?"

Update your rating of above items again, if required

Write your Resolution for New Year.

My Resolution for Year .... is

....

Part 3

1. Clearly, specify the outcomes of the resolution.
2. **Break it down into 5 goals,**

- Your first goal (an immediately achievable goal) with a target of first 10 days of the new year.
- Your second goal should have a target of first 45 days of the new year.
- Your third goal should have a target of first 100 days of the new year.

- ◦ Your fourth goal should have a target of first 200 days of the new year
- ◦ your fifth and last goal should have the target of first 300 days of the year.

1. Each of the goals must have clearly specified results to be achieved, and its deadline (with date and time). You need to make a chart for it.

My Goals

• Specify the results to be achieved for the five goals of your New Year Resolution.

• With each goal specify its deadline

Part 4

For the first goal, you must specify the immediate actions you need to take to get the results in first 10 days.

- a. Specify the decisions you need to take.
- b. Specify the actions you need to take.
- c. Specify the behavioral changes you would require.
- d. Specify the rules you need to strictly follow with complete discipline.
- e. Specify the rewards for following the rules and getting the results.
- f. Specify the punishment for not following the rules and getting the results. [Your specification of the punishment should not be damaging in any way for anyone, including yoursel It is to remind your mind about the importance of following the rules and getting the results. The final objective is to make you sincere about following the rules and being in the

discipline.]

g. Specify the first action for your resolution, which you are going to take on the first day of the year.

Part 5

4. As soon as you get success in your first goal you need to write the immediate actions which you must take to get success in your second goal, by getting the desired results.
5. You need to keep doing it for goals third, fourth and fifth.
6. Answer "What outcomes I am expecting from my pre-resolution actions?"
7. What actions do I need to take? Write down your pre-resolution actions for gaining the momentum, before the start of the new year. (The objective is to make you start work on your resolution much before the start of the year so that when you enter the year you are already in speed towards your goals.]
8. Now, take your first decided action immediately, without thinking much about it.

CHAPTER TEN

Is my resolution correct

Test your resolution.

Once you have identified the NY resolution, it should be verified for its genuineness. It can be tested by answering few questions.

- What is my New Year Resolution?

- What are the reasons to choose this resolution? Why not any other?

- How would my life be affected, if I do not follow this resolution?

- What outcomes am I expecting out of it?

- What challenges would I be facing to follow this resolution?

- Am I prepared to take on the challenges?

- What will make me leave my resolution?

- How can I ensure that I follow my resolution, in any condition?

- Am I enthusiastic about it and looking forward to it?

Use SMART Criteria:

You should also test your NYR on the SMART Criteria. For each segment of the SMART criteria, you need to rate your resolution on the scale of 1 to 10 with 1 as minimum and 10 as maximum.

Let us understand the SMART criteria.

To make sure your goals are clear and reachable, each one should be:

Specific - Your New Year's resolution must be very specific and clearly defined. It should not be too vague or broad, for example, "I want to improve my health", instead you should be very specific, for example, "I would lose 20 pounds of my weight by the end-of-the-year". Your New Year's Resolutions should also be significant, sensible, and simple.

Measurable: Your new year resolutions should be measurable. It means that you should be able to master the outcomes or the results, which you want to achieve from your actions for resolutions. For example, "I would like to earn a $10,000 in passive income by end-of-the-year". Your New Year's Resolution should also be meaningful and motivating.

Achievable: The New Year's Resolution which you are making should also be achievable and sensible. You should not set the bar so high that it looks unachievable and irrational. The objective of your resolution is to take powerful actions to achieve a specific outcome. If your goals are irrational then you would not be able to take any action towards it.

Results-focused: Your actions for your New Year's Resolutions should be results based, reasonable and realistic. It means that you should be having clearly defined results and outcomes for your resolutions. The clarity of results definition is directly proportional to the strength of actions and focus on energy.

Timely (*Time-bound*) - You should have clearly defined guidelines for the goals of your New Year's Resolutions. To achieve results in time, you must specify the deadlines for it. Even if your final goal is broken down into several sub-goals, you must have the specified deadlines of getting results for each of them.

SMART Criteria

You should test your New Year's Resolution on the SMART Criteria. For each segment of

the SMART criteria, you need to rate your resolution on the scale of 1 to 10 with 1 as

minimum and 10 as a maximum.

If your total Rating in SMART Criteria is more than 35 (70%) then your resolution is genuine

and correct.

The necessary elements to make your New Year's resolution

<u>Clarity about your needs</u>- The first and most important element to make your New Year's resolution is to have a complete clarity about the needs. It means that you must know that what you want, and why you want it. Your needs must have an emotional connection to make you feel

motivated for taking hard decisions and actions.

It needs to be **practical and achievable**- Your needs must be practical and achievable, otherwise they would make no sense. If you want to act towards succeeding in your New Year's Resolutions, then you must be rational for setting your resolutions and goals.

The feeling of strong need for the **outcomes** of your actions- The outcomes of your actions and their connection with your emotions is important for taking powerful actions.

Belief in self that you will follow through-You need to have belief in yourself that you will be able to take the required decisions and actions for achieving success in your New Year's Resolutions. It is important that without belief you will never get success in your goals.

External conditions supporting you – You need to be sensible enough to identify your New Year's Resolutions which are achievable, with the external conditions supporting your actions. For example, you want to jog every morning in open but it rains every alternate day, affecting your regularity. In that case, you must be having an indoor place for you to jog regularly.

Essentials to follow through your New Year's Resolution

Emotional connection with your resolution- Without the emotional connection, it is difficult to feel motivated.

Preparing for it- The actions for your New Year's Resolutions will not be magical. You must prepare for it. For example, if you want to get physically fit then you must be having the access to required training and equipment for physical exercises.

Starting early- This is an important component to follow through in your New Year's Resolution, but most of the people miss it. You must start early to act on your resolutions. It means that even before the start of New Year, you must start to act on your resolution, to gain momentum.

Being internally-driven rather than externally-driven- Your energy for your New Year's resolution must be from inside not from outside. You can be a part of a group, but your motivation for your resolution must come from inside. It can be the passion for results or commitment towards your goals.

Discipline- Every result, ever achieved has discipline attached to it. Without discipline, we cannot get quality results in any area or domain.

Commitment– For the success of NYR we must have the necessary sincerity for taking the hard actions and persevere.

Belief in self- Till we believe our abilities and competencies to do something, we will not be able to achieve anything.

Feedback: You need to consistently take feedback for your actions and results and make the required improvements to better action next time.

Strategies to keep your resolution

Strategies to keep your resolution, till you achieve it:

Clarity - Be very clear about the actions you need to take and results you must achieve. You should also know about "What I will do?" and "What I will not do?"

Emotional connection- Emotional connection is a necessary component for enjoying your actions and to have the necessary commitment towards it.

Focus on results - Your focus needs to be on the results to be achieved, not just on taking the actions. It is important to understand that you must enjoy your journey towards your goals through actions and decisions, in addition to the pleasure from the results.

Commitment to meet the deadlines- You must be committed to meet the deadlines, which you have set for your goals, because if you miss the deadlines, then it would affect your results.

Daily remember your why- Create a reminder system to consistently remember your 'Why'. You must create a system which can help you to get the daily motivation for actions. You need to daily remember the 'Why' for your New Year's Resolution.

Create a daily ritual - You can also create a daily ritual for connecting with your resolution. For example, if your NYR is to get peace of mind, then you should meditate for few minutes every morning, just after waking up.

Use reward and punishment - Reward and punishment have been proven to be effective in organizational perspective, according to human resource managers. You can utilize the similar technique to keep your New Year's Resolution. You can reward yourselves for achieving results, and accept punishments for not keeping the commitments. We need to remember that the punishment has to be mild and not damaging in any way.

Associate yourself with a group of people with similar resolution- You can also find people with similar resolution and associate yourselves with them. For example, if you want to improve your health then you can join a group of joggers, who also have the similar goals of improving their health. Even though it is an external force, but it can be a good addition to your internal strength.

Take help from your family and friends: to become your partner in your resolutions. They will make you achieve it. Your family and friends care about you and are always ready to help. You should take support from them for helping you to enforce the rules for your resolution. They can keep you disciplined for your actions.

CHAPTER ELEVEN

Develop "Resolution Mindset"

In this section, we will discuss some powerful techniques for making and keeping your New Year Resolution.

Resolution mindset is a process of orienting the mind towards making the commitments for the new year and keeping them. Here, we have specified several techniques and strategies which will act as a bridge to develop the "resolution mindset".

To ensure the quality of results your actions must be backed by beliefs, emotions, and logical reasoning. If any of these elements is missing, then it would be difficult to put sincere efforts towards your resolution.

Let us discuss the techniques, which will develop the "resolution mindset".

Prepare early for NYR: Make it a big event for the start of the year. In fact, you should be starting the actions on your resolution much before the start of new year. It is about getting the initial momentum before entering 2018. We have utilized this technique in our methodology, discussed in this book.

Seriousness: Make a resolution only when you are serious about it. Take the specified test in the workbook to check your seriousness level about making the resolution and keeping it.

Replace all 'should' with 'must': You must take a commitment to follow your NYR, otherwise it is a waste of time and efforts.

Only one: Make only one NYR and follow it strictly. You should allow yourself to move to next resolution, only after you have successfully completed the previous one, with required outcomes.

Control: Focus on something which is in your control, not controlled by external forces. If your New Year's resolution is dependent on the mood and actions of other people, then the probability of keeping your resolution is less. Your resolution is your responsibility, not anybody else's. You need to take charge and drive yourself through your internal strength, rather than anything external.

Start small: You need to start small with your resolution and slowly strengthen it. Your initial focus must be to get early results, however small. It will allow you to get motivation for moving forward towards bigger goals of your resolution.

Start immediately: It is an important step to take action on your New Year's Resolution. You need to decide on a specific goal and start immediately. Most of the people who delay their actions on their New Year's Resolution lose their motivation for moving forward. Till we taste initial success with early results, we may get difficulties in keeping the discipline.

Invest time: Make it a serious affair by investing time (i.e. completing the workbook, planning, starting early) and money to it. It is a natural psychology of human beings, that if we invest something on some specific area, it rises in value. That is the reason that you should be investing your time and efforts for making the resolution and preparing for it.

SMARTresolution: Use SMART methodology and criteria for setting goals. We have discussed it in the previous section of the book. It means that your New Year's Resolution should be specific, measurable, achievable, result-focused/ realistic and timely.

Only one: Make only one resolution not many, as they will stretch your focus and efforts. You can create a list of your New Year's Resolutions but must arrange them based on their priority. Start with only one and achieve it successfully. You can move on to next after achieving results for the first resolution.

Clear and specific: Most of the failed resolutions lack clarity in the outcomes and actions. That is the reason that people are unable to follow them. Be very clear and specific about your resolution. The clearer you are about your needs and commitment, the better would be your focus, and effective would be your efforts.

New Area: Do not take any topic in which you have failed in the past, instead take a new and fresh topic. Areas in which you have failed once may have some negative emotions attached to it. Start something new and fresh.

Anticipate problems and identify solutions: You should anticipate the problems which could pop up while following your NYR. You should identify all of them and find solutions and action to be taken. Also, you must identify a step by step process for taking action, if something unexpected happens. You must ensure that in any condition your resolution is not weakened, in any way.

Create rituals: Make few rituals to act on NYR regularly. To bring regularity in your specific area you should create rituals, which you follow strictly. For example, many religions have early morning prayers, which are considered as powerful & deep. It compels people to wake up early in the morning. To make sure that you act on your resolution regularly, you need to create some specific ritual and consistently follow it.

Get accountability: Make your well-wishers and the people caring for you enforce accountability, for keeping your NYR. It means that you allow your family members and close friends to become the part of your New Year's Resolution. These people will keep pushing you towards your resolution, to make sure that you get benefit out of it.

Set deadlines: You need to set deadlines for achieving resolution results. Deadlines are specified in time, by which a specific task must be completed. For example, if a project has a deadline of next Monday at 5 PM, then it means that the project must be completed before 5 PM on Monday. Deadlines act in a unique way as they set a specific target to be achieved. The best way to achieve a deadline is to create sub-deadlines, in which the final goal is divided into several sub-goals, with their own individual deadlines. These smaller deadlines would lead to the main deadline.

Meditation: To achieve a specific goal you need to meditate on it every morning and before sleeping in the night. It means that your resolution must be the first thought, which should come to your mind when you wake up early in the morning, and the last thought before going to sleep. It will orient you towards your resolution, by keeping it at the top of your mind.

Initial success: To get the final results in your New Year's Resolution you should break down your goals into smaller parts, with clearly specified results. It is logical to start with easier tasks with shorter deadlines. Achieving results will motivate you. You must get initial successes, however small.

Rewards and punishment: It is the most common method, which is used by corporations around the world. They reward for the success and results and punish for the failures. You can utilize the same methodology, for achieving results for your resolution. You can reward yourself for getting the success in your sub-goals, and set punishment for not achieving them. You need to understand that the meaning of punishment here is only to remind yourself of the importance of goals. It should not hurt you, physically or mentally, in any way. For example, the punishment for not achieving a subgoal can be to cancel your weekend pizza.

Small commitments: Before starting full-fledged for your resolution you need to warm up, just the way you loosen your muscles before starting your physical exercises. You should take some smaller commitments, which are comparatively easier, and you must follow them. For example, the New Year's Resolution for getting regularity in your physical exercises, you can start with five minutes physical exercises, then you can slowly move to 10 minutes and so on.

Change the name: Most of the people have tried for years to make resolutions and keep them. After several years of failing in their New Year's Resolutions, people tend to see it as a failed project. If that is the case, then you should not be calling it as the New Year's Resolution, instead, you should call it by a different name, to bring freshness to the project. You can be creative in identifying interesting names for your New Year's Resolution. Some examples can be NY commitment, NY shake-up, NY revolution, NY renewal, NY transformation or NY reformation.

Group activity: When we work with other people on a specific project, then everyone becomes accountable for every other's success. It would be great if you could team up with other people with similar NY Resolutions, to make it a group activity.

Daily routine: Your daily routine is the part of your habit. If you attach your actions for NYR to one of your daily routine, then it would become the part or extension of that activity. It would not require any extra effort to do it. For example, if you have decided to read twelve books in a year, but you do not get the time for it, you can find the solution in one of your daily routines. If you could start to listen to audio books while you exercise, which is your daily routine, then you would get success in your resolution, and even continue it for years to come.

Be happy: Many times, the pressure to follow the resolution makes it stressful and unexciting. This is one of the most common reason resisting actions, for New Year's Resolution. You must make sure that you attach happiness, satisfaction, and fulfillment to your resolutions. Never let negative feeling get attached to it. You need to become your advocate for New Year's Resolutions.

Respect it: You must have observed many people making fun of their New Year's Resolutions as if they already knew about their inability to follow it. You must respect your resolutions, then only you can follow its course. You should neither yourself nor allow anybody else, to make fun of your New Year's Resolutions. You need to understand that your New Year's Resolution is yours, as it was created by you and finally going to affect you. Any disrespect to your goals, commitments or resolutions is the disrespect to your image and identity.

Be persistent- Persistence is the power of successful human beings, which never allow them to accept defeat. You need to be persistent in your New Year's Resolution. It is possible that you fail occasionally, but you need to rise and start again. You must keep doing it, till you get the required outcomes.

Never be complacent: Complacency crops up when you take an activity casually. Your actions become casual if you are not serious about a specific task. It is a known fact that anything done without sincerity, will not lead to results. You must make sure that your New Year's Resolution is among the top priority in your life. Soon, your actions would become the part of your habit.

Analyze: You should analyze and take the challenge only if you are serious about the required change, which you want to bring through your New Year's resolution. If you are not committed to it, then do not do it.

Get freshness: The activities involved in your New Year's resolution should be new and innovative, giving you the feeling of freshness. If it is the repetition of anything stale and boring, then it would be difficult to get excited about it.

Get support: If you require any guidance or support from anyone else, then do not hesitate to ask for it. You need to make sure that the other person is genuine and is ready to help. It also makes you more engaged with your New Year's Resolution.

Simplicity: Try to keep the actions for your New Year's Resolution as simple as possible. In fact, your New Year's Resolution must also be simple. Make sure that you do not add any complexity to the required actions so that you can continue it without much preparation or thinking. Your objective should keep your actions normal and natural, without any pressure or stress.

Words: This point is also an extension of simplicity. Our minds understand ideas and concepts with words. Complexity in words may create confusion, while usage of simple words would make the understanding of the idea, simple. The New Year's Resolution and its actions must be explained in simple words and plain language.

Write down: Your New Year's Resolution should not just remain in your mind, in the form of a thought. You must write it down on a piece of paper or digitally in clear and simple words. You will understand the power of writing, once you do it.

Modification: It is possible that once you are in the new year, you realize that your New Year's Resolution was not exactly the way you wanted it. It would be a long wait for next year to recreate NY Resolution and act on it. Instead, you can modify your present resolution to suit your requirements. It is to be noted that you should not be changing your resolution more than once.

Make it cool: Everybody loves cool people and cool things. You should also make your New Year's Resolution cool and interesting. For example, physical exercises can be an aerobic dance with music.

Convince logically: Humans are different from animals, mainly due to their mind and emotions. We use logic to understand the value of an action or an event. You must use logic to convince yourselves of your New Year's Resolution. Until you are completely convinced, you will not be able to put your full force and sincerity towards it. Self-argue and clear all the doubts and confusions, regarding your New Year Resolution.

Emotional connection: It is an important element in the actions and decisions of human beings. It brings sincerity and strength to the actions of an individual. You should pause for some time to get into the skin of the New Year's Resolution so that you are truly connected with it. Once the emotional connection with your New Year's Resolution is established, then everything would fall into place.

Rise Higher: Never allow people to put you down or demotivate you. You should control your emotional state and motivation. If you can master this skill, then your performance in actions would rise dramatically.

Keep Growing: You must experience growth in your actions towards New Year's Resolution. Growth is a good motivator. Grow and help others in their life and work.

CHAPTER TWELVE

List of New Year Resolutions

2017 most common New Year Resolutions

Based on the google searches

- Get healthy
- Get organized
- Live life to fullest
- Learn new hobbies
- Spend less/ Save more
- Travel
- Read More

List of resolutions

- Lose weight- exercise more/ get in shape/ improve health/ develop healthy habits
- Travel more
- Quit smoking

- Get full body checkup
- Listen to music more
- Reduce consumption of fast food
- Stop judging people
- Stop procrastination
- Improve concentration and mental skills
- Meet new people
- Become more active
- Become more confident
- Take more responsibilities
- Take more initiations
- Earn more money
- Become more polite
- Stop being angry
- Reduce stress
- Learn to be happy in life
- Get more quality sleep
- Watch less TV
- Read more
- Find a significant other
- Become more stylish
- Spend more time with people that matter
- Moderate drinking or quit drinking
- Get out of debt
- Learn a new language
- Volunteer and give more to charity
- Learn to forgive
- Learn new skill
- Develop a new hobby
- Get freedom from the grudges
- Adopt a pet
- Become more organized
- Learn to cook

- Reinvent yourself
- Become punctual
- Earn from your hobby
- Bring emotions under control
- Spend less time on social media
- Become more productive
- Manage time better
- Learn the art to defend yourself (physically/ verbally)
- Improve communication skills
- Make your loved ones feel special
- Reconnect with family and friends
- Become more innovative
- Become a troubleshooter
- Start to express yourself creatively
- Face your fears and insecurities
- Start to write
- Learn and start to meditate
- Play more
- Eat fewer calories
- Start something new
- Be more grateful
- Discover your dreams/ passion and act on them
- Spend more time with nature
- Enjoy little things
- Improve your IQ and EQ
- Bring more peace to life
- Be more kind
- Be more positive
- Start a blog and post regularly

Unleash the Power from your Resolutions
Now, you are ready to Unleash the Power of your New Year Resolution.

You can also use this process to get success in your other resolutions.

After several iterations of success in your resolutions, you would have your own personalized system to generate value from your Resolutions, including New Year's Resolutions.

All the Best.

About Authors

NILAM PATHAK

Nilam Pathak is a communication professional who has worked with global organizations and institutions to realize the potential of corporate employees, students and masses. She believes in the power of Personality Development and Communication Skills to empower the vulnerable.

She has trained professionals and trainers of various domains and nations. She is an internationally published author of eight books.

https://direct.me/nilam

ANSHUMAN SHARMA

Anshuman is an entrepreneur and investor and has been instrumental in nurturing many successful companies. He has created several profitable companies in various domains. He is also involved in supporting the development of several other organizations. In business, his interests lie in cutting-edge technologies and innovative services.

His guidance has helped many businessmen, investors, and entrepreneurs to succeed in their objectives. He has also supported several entrepreneurship cells and incubation centers.